YOUR KNOWLEDGE HAS VALUE

- We will publish your bachelor's and master's thesis, essays and papers

- Your own eBook and book - sold worldwide in all relevant shops

- Earn money with each sale

Upload your text at www.GRIN.com
and publish for free

Mario Nsonga

Moral Hero and Immoral World: A Study of Ethics in "Watchmen"

GRIN Verlag

Bibliografische Information der Deutschen Nationalbibliothek:

Die Deutsche Bibliothek verzeichnet diese Publikation in der Deutschen National-bibliografie; detaillierte bibliografische Daten sind im Internet über http://dnb.d-nb.de/ abrufbar.

Dieses Werk sowie alle darin enthaltenen einzelnen Beiträge und Abbildungen sind urheberrechtlich geschützt. Jede Verwertung, die nicht ausdrücklich vom Urheberrechtsschutz zugelassen ist, bedarf der vorherigen Zustimmung des Verlages. Das gilt insbesondere für Vervielfältigungen, Bearbeitungen, Übersetzungen, Mikroverfilmungen, Auswertungen durch Datenbanken und für die Einspeicherung und Verarbeitung in elektronische Systeme. Alle Rechte, auch die des auszugsweisen Nachdrucks, der fotomechanischen Wiedergabe (einschließlich Mikrokopie) sowie der Auswertung durch Datenbanken oder ähnliche Einrichtungen, vorbehalten.

Imprint:

Copyright © 2011 GRIN Verlag GmbH
Druck und Bindung: Books on Demand GmbH, Norderstedt Germany
ISBN: 978-3-656-35423-9

This book at GRIN:

http://www.grin.com/en/e-book/207834/moral-hero-and-immoral-world-a-study-of-ethics-in-watchmen

GRIN - Your knowledge has value

Der GRIN Verlag publiziert seit 1998 wissenschaftliche Arbeiten von Studenten, Hochschullehrern und anderen Akademikern als eBook und gedrucktes Buch. Die Verlagswebsite www.grin.com ist die ideale Plattform zur Veröffentlichung von Hausarbeiten, Abschlussarbeiten, wissenschaftlichen Aufsätzen, Dissertationen und Fachbüchern.

Visit us on the internet:

http://www.grin.com/

http://www.facebook.com/grincom

http://www.twitter.com/grin_com

Mario V. Nsonga
Studiengang: American Studies (B.A.)

Moral Hero and Immoral World: A Study of Ethics in *Watchmen*
by
Mario V. Nsonga

Department of English and Linguistics
American Comics
28 February 2011

Table of Contents

1. Introduction — 3
2. Rorschach: Psychotic Killer or Hero in Disguise — 3
3. Veidt: Megalomaniac Genius or Desperate Gambler? — 10
4. Conclusion — 16
5. Works Cited — 17

1. Introduction

Watchmen belongs to the most complex comics ever published by DC Comics and tackles a grand variety of themes on a tectonical level. This paper will particular shed light on the actions and conduct of Veidt and Rorschach. By doing so, it will discuss whether their behavior is – according to our Western system of values - morally and ethically sustainable. Another question this paper will touch upon is to which degree both characters deconstruct our *classical* notion of the superhero.

2. Rorschach: Psychotic Killer or Hero in Disguise?

Despite adhering to the protagonists in the comic "Watchmen", Rorschach simultaneously represents one of the most ambiguous and complex characters. His struggle for the good implies the deployment of torture, violent interrogations and other atrocious actions. Hence, the rise of the question whether Rorschach's unorthodox methods are justified in order to "punish the evil" (Chapter 1, p. 24, fig. 6) and disseminate the good are more than intelligible. But are his actions morally and ethically acceptable or do they actually come into conflict with our notion of morality. And furthermore, do they undermine our "classical conception of the superhero"?

According to the definition of Peter Coogan a superhero is as followed

A heroic character with a selfless, pro-social mission; with superpowers – extraordinary abilities, advanced technology, or highly physical, mental, or mystical skills; who has a superhero identity embodied in a codename and iconic costume, which typically express his biography, character, powers, or origin (transformation from ordinary person to superhero); and who is generically distinct [...] by a preponderance of generic conventions (Coogan 77).

"The plot is structured around his [Rorschach's] investigation of several murders" (Loftis 67). His first station in the process of his investigations leads him to the bar where Rorschach reveals his high potential of aggression by using the provocative man (cf. Chapter 1, p. 15, fig. 7) as "mere mean" (Nuttall 94) to interrogate the audience which he perceives as "cockroaches" (Chapter 1, p. 10, fig. 9). He does not hesitate to use fear and violence as demonstrative instruments of his power and superiority:

(Chapter 1, p. 16, fig. 4, 6, 9)

Therefore, Rorschach reveals already at this early stage of the plot development a *consequentialist* attitude since "he believes that [his] actions should be judged by their consequences, implying that the ends will sometimes justify the means" (Loftis 64) – in that case the disclosure of Edward Blake's murder. Furthermore despite his violent interrogation at the bar, the breach into the apartment of Dreiberg (cf. Chapter 1, p. 10, fig. 4 ff.) and the military residence of Dr. Manhattan (cf. Chapter 1, p. 19, fig. 1 ff.), Rorschach – at least according to Immanuel Kant (cf. Loftis 71) – still remains a moral (anti-) hero since he possesses the "will to do good" (71): warning the others of a masked killer and the arrest of the perpetrator. Rorschach separates good and evil and adheres fervently to this "dichotomous thinking" (72) which simultaneously highlights his "failure to recognize the intrinsic value of persons" (72) and his inability to change stance. When Moloch explains Rorschach that he is "not Moloch anymore" (Chapter 2, p. 21, fig. 4), but a "retired businessman" (Chapter 2, p. 21, fig. 3), Rorschach is not willing and not able to believe him since according to his world conception if one has been once evil, one will always remain evil – and "evil must be punished" (Chapter 1, p. 24, fig. 6). Again, "Rorschach slips into a consequentialist reasoning in order to justify a hyper masculine display of power and violence" (Loftis 72). His struggle for justice is morally marginal since it often appears as if Rorschach's main focus does not necessarily lay in the well-being of society but rather in the satisfaction of his own psycho-sadistic bloodlust for *justice* (cf. Chapter 6, p.23, fig. 1 ff.) which contradicts the classical notion of the superhero who acts unselfish, pro-social – and sometimes even altruistic – to preserve law and order (cf. Coogan 77 ff.). In the next vital scene, Rorschach falls into a trap and is arrested by the law enforcement – but not after exorbitant resistance:

(Chapter 5, p. 26, fig. 4; p. 27, fig. 1, 4)

Whereas *Superman*, the undisputed superhero, is admired by society and befriended with the local police forces, Rorschach clearly represents his counterpart, is wanted by the federal government and definitely incorporates the unpopular anti-hero (cf. Chapter 5, p. 28, fig. 5 ff.). But to which degree do we perceive Rorschach's aggression and unorthodox acts as a violation of our Western conceptionalization of good will and moral virtues? "The [...] error is the belief that violence is a natural and inevitable expression of ill-will, and non-violence of good-will, and that violence is therefore intrinsically evil and non-violence intrinsically good" (Niebuhr 172). On that account, we as the readers, feel compassion and empathy with the apparently misunderstood and lonely antihero since Rorschach "impress[es] us with [his] heroic intentions and devotion but at the same time disturb[s] us with [his] moral extremism" (White 79). Moreover, our sympathy develops further when we learn about

Rorschach's grow up – devoid of any maternal love (cf. Chapter 6, p.3, fig. 2 ff.): his mother being a prostitute and revealing a similar violent character trait. The domestic and physical violence he sustained during his childhood

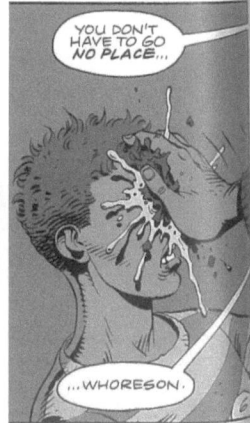

(Chapter 6, p. 4, fig. 6, 7; p. 6, fig. 9)

transformed Rorschach into a "psychopathic vigilante" (White 79) with a strong elaborated apathetic charisma since he stores all his pain, disillusionment and aggressions inside:

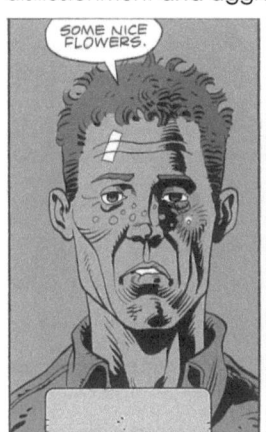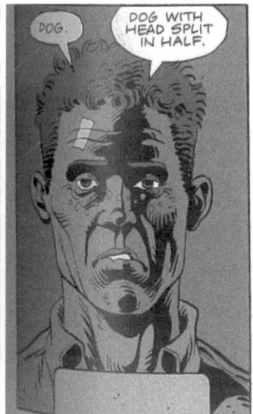

(Chapter 6, p. 5, fig. 2; p. 6, fig. 5; p. 17, fig. 7)

Consequently, his "dichotomous thinking" and misanthropic world perception are reinforced by his background and he begins to see the world in black and white, or more figuratively in suffering and salvation. His strict black-and-white-value-system and inability to perceive the *grey shades* explains the choice of his black and white mask as he states himself: "Black and white. Moving. Changing. Not mixing. No gray" (Chapter 6, p. 10, fig. 3) and furthermore underlines his regrettable biography.

Moreover, Rorschach is depicted as the "unkempt, taciturn, [laconic]" (Loftis 70) hardliner who "even in the face of Armageddon [...] shall not compromise" (Chapter 1, p. 24, fig. 6) in punishing the evil:

(Chapter 1, p. 24, fig. 6)

According to Loftis, "Rorschach [...] appears to be a deontologist" (Loftis 64) since he does not "think of morality in terms of ends and means" (64), but acts "only in ways that express essential moral rules" (64), i. e. Rorschach does not conceive a rational master plan to "promote happiness" (66), but rather acts on a more emotional level to do "the right thing" (64) in a particular, instantaneous situation. So it is only natural for Rorschach to "punish" the alleged kidnapper of the 6-year-old girl by splitting the brains of the owner's dogs, strapping him at the heater and torching the whole building:

(Chapter 6, p. 17, fig. 6; p. 24, fig. 8; p. 25, fig. 7)

Again, the death of the man does not fulfill any multipurpose, but rather stresses Rorschach's deontological need for "doing the right thing" (Loftis 64). But does not Rorschach's killing contradict our Western notion of morality and ethics? According to the utilitarianist point of view, "only goodwill is intrinsically good" (Niebuhr 173) and "as soon as goodwill expresses itself in specific actions, it must be determined whether the right motive has chosen the right instruments for the attainment of its goal and whether the objective is a defensible one" (173). If utilitarianism implies "respect for the life" (173) and prohibition of "violence to the fellowman's life" (173) than Rorschach has definitely acted immoral and ethically on a not justifiable level. On the other hand, the man gives away that he has nothing to do "with that little girl" (cf. Chapter 6, p. 24, fig. 7), revealing his insight about Rorschach's visit and insinuating to his potential guilt:

(Chapter 6, p. 24, fig. 7)

It expeditiously becomes evident that moral judgment and the justice cause are not imperatively "mutually exclusive" (Niebuhr 257), "but neither are they easily harmonized" (257). The character of Rorschach incarnates the extended executive organ of justice which in some cases can only be implemented by suppressing – at least temporarily – the faculty for rational morality. Nite Owl and Rorschach finally discover Veidt's genocidal *master plan* and as subsequent reaction Rorschach "deontologically rationalizes his actions, such as stabbing away at Veidt using anything he can find, even though he knows he can't succeed" (Loftis 64) since Veidt is physically and mentally superior to him:

(Chapter 11, p. 18, fig. 8; p. 19, fig. 1, 7)

Anyway, after Veidt has successfully completed his plot to murder millions of people to "usher in an age of illumination so dazzling that humanity will reject the darkness in its heart" (Loftis 67), Rorschach is the only one who abstains from concealing Veidt's action (cf. Chapter 12, p. 20, fig. 8). Whereby lying would in that case be "morally required" (Nuttall 94) since the revelation of truth "would destroy any chance of peace, dooming earth to worse destruction" (Chapter 12, p. 20, fig. 4) as explains Dr. Manhattan. According to Kant's *imperative*, Rorschach's intention to disseminate the truth is morally totally correct (cf. Nuttall 94), thus Rorschach's atomization by Dr. Manhattan (cf. Chapter 12, p. 24, fig. 4) can be seen as act of martyrdom since he dies for the *just cause* – at least seen from a Kantian moral-philosophical perspective. Furthermore, "if the truth becomes known to the public through Rorschach's morally valid actions, we can't hold him responsible for the consequences" (96). From the utilitarian perspective which focuses "on the result of actions, rather than on the actions themselves" (96), the question whether Rorschach should keep silent as well, depends on the outcome of those two possibilities, choosing the one which would maximize world's happiness (cf. Loftis 68), even though the choice could contradict with society's "highest moral ideal" (Niebuhr 257): justice. Subsequently, Rorschach exemplifies the moral hero in a modern, complex and sinister world, albeit he does not fulfill the classical conventions of a superhero like e.g. Superman would do.

3. Veidt: Megalomaniac Genius or Desperate Gambler?

At first glance, Veidt seems to represent the absolute counterpart of Rorschach: cultivated, eloquent and charismatic. However, in the process of the story his vicious genocidal master plan is revealed and a thoroughly investigation shows surprisingly Veidt's similarities with Rorschach concerning his ethical worldview and moral extremism. But is Veidt's scheme of establishing a *New World Order* morally and ethically acceptable? And if so, could we still call him a classical hero?

White depicts Veidt as "the megalomaniac genius" (White 79) who "believes that all actions should be judged by their consequences, implying that the ends will sometimes justify the means" (Loftis 64). Hence, Veidt represents per se the incarnation of the utilitarian philosophy which justifies morally questionable actions as long as "they do [not] produce the reverse of happiness" (66). But who is Veidt to be able to judge whether the sacrifice of millions of New Yorker lives will in the aftermath "maximize happiness for all" (66)? Already the choice of his superhero named "Ozymandias" discloses Veidt's *pharaonic-godlike* disturbed self-perception, drawing his inspiration from Alexander the Great. He as *the smartest man on the planet* simply feels chosen "to take the weight of that awful, necessary crime" to "save humanity":

(Chapter 12, p.27, fig. 2)

Therefore it is crucial to take a closer look at the beginning of the story to grasp Veidt's motives and judging his actions from a moral perspective.

In the first chapter, Rorschach visits Veidt in order to discuss Blake's decease. Eye-catching is Veidt's theatrical behavior towards Rorschach and the death of the Comedian, acting as if he were authentically worried and contemplating about the death of the Comedian:

(Chapter 1, p. 17, fig. 3, 6, 8)

Veidt turns out to be a proper *luminary of hypocrisy*, suggesting the assassination – which he performed himself - could have been "a political killing" (Chapter 1, p. 17, fig. 3). According to the Kantian philosophy in which lying, implying hypocrisy, is "never permissible" (Nuttall 93), Veidt acts already at this early stage of the plot immoral since he lies consciously to Rorschach although he knows the truth. Afterwards, he appears at the Comedian's funeral and represents his consolations to his former partners (cf. Chapter 2, p. 19, fig. 5, 6) – extending his performance in the public. Interestingly enough, we as readers can yet hardly imagine that such an *angel-like* looking creature with *pure, innocent* blue eyes and blond hair will later unveil itself accountable for all the murders. Again, Kant's imperative gains a foothold and highlights Veidt's intriguing conduct as essentially wrong since his former partners represent "rational agents" (Nuttall 93) who are of "absolute worth" (93) - like all human beings - and by manipulating them, Veidt treats them as "mere means" (94), "rather than as beings who possess an inviolable dignity" (93) to implement his murderous scheme. On the other hand, we should acknowledge two vital facts: Firstly, Veidt is not *Kantian*, but - as already aforementioned - rather incorporates the utilitarian philosophy. Secondly, acting morally *adequately* – at least according to our Western system of values - would not only compel Veidt to tell the truth and reveal his insane enterprise but simultaneously very likely undermine his "dream of perpetual peace and brotherhood for human society" (Niebuhr 21). In order to attain that goal, Veidt demonstrates a sinister "willingness to make big sacrifices for even bigger ends, and to gamble on probabilities" (Loftis 65) when he assigns his own assassination, putting his own life in serious jeopardy and accepting the death of innocent people, in that case his secretary, just to divert suspicion from himself:

(Chapter 5, p. 13, fig. 8; p. 14, fig. 1, 3)

"The potential for consequentialism to promote rationalization is obvious: once one starts in making sacrifices and trade-offs, it gets easy to make the sacrifices that will serve one's own interest" (Loftis 67). Having killed the Comedian (cf. Chapter 1, p. 2, fig. 3 ff.), his three servants (cf. Chapter 11, p. 11, fig. 7 ff.) and his favorite genetically engineered cat Bubastis to prevent Dr. Manhattan from thwarting the execution of his project (cf. Chapter 12, p. 14, fig. 4) – or as he would call it *sacrificed* them for *a greater good* - Veidt reveals a pretty *consequentialist* attitude as well:

(Chapter 11, p. 12, fig. 5; Chapter 12, p. 14, fig. 4)

In fact, it does not much differ from Rorschach's: both have the inherited "desire to do right" (Niebuhr 37) with the sole deviation in their interpretation of the role of punishment. According to Veidt, "punishment is only a good policy if, as a consequence, it makes someone happier by preventing future crime" (Loftis 66) whereas in Rorschach's case all "evil must [intransigently] be punished" (Chapter 1, p. 24, fig. 6). Consequently, Veidt repeatedly transgresses the non-utilitarian reader's notion of a *moral hero* and eventually becomes the "tragic villain, a man whose overwhelming ego and failure to appreciate the dark nature of life led him to think the end can sometimes justify the means" (Loftis 70). And thus he sacrifices with ease millions of lives (cf. Chapter 12, p. 1 ff.), "using [them] as tools for ending the Cold War, thus violating their [people's] rights as persons" (Loftis 70) – e.g. something the anti-ideology-imposing *Superman* would have never done! However, according to the utilitarian philosophy Veidt's actions are still morally justifiable as long as these "actions are right in proportion as they tend to promote happiness" (66). Indeed, Veidt plans to maximize happiness in the world (cf. 66) since he believes that without sacrifice and a *Watchman*, "society [would] never be sufficiently intelligent to bring all power under its control" (Niebuhr 21) which basically represents a morally goodwill. Concerning the ethical point of view, one has to grasp that "the destruction of [...] life or the suppression of freedom result in the immediate destruction of moral values" (171). We notice that ethics and moral do seldom go hand in hand, they sometimes even mutually exclude. Veidt's megalomaniac plan to "take over the world" (Loftis 67) eventually succeeds. However, the reader first becomes witness of Veidt's celebration of his own glory, displaying an exorbitant amount of selfishness and self-assertion – again something the unselfish and altruistic Superman would never do - since the glory rather reinforces his ego than being of direct use for society:

(Chapter 12, p. 19, fig. 7)

Veidt is no superhero – to be more specifically even though his heroic intentions might be of most noble nature – the attainment of his goals definitely destroys our classical conceptualization of the (super-) hero and his actions transgress our system of moral and ethical values, thus rendering Veidt into the villain of the story.

4. Conclusion

As the previous chapters underline, the question whether our two protagonists act morally and ethically in accordance with our Western system of values cannot be answered with a simply *yes* or *no* since both have the "desire to do right" (Niebuhr 37). Both attempt to control the world's destiny, both believe that their consequentialist-utilitarianist worldview and conduct suffice to grasp and shape reality, and both parties express a high willingness to make big sacrifice. Rorschach's dichotomous thinking limits his ability to perceive the *grey shades* and to finally compromise with Veidt. Thus Rorschach sacrifices his life for his moral values, rendering him a hero – at least a moral one. Veidt has lost his believe humanity would ever lead a peaceful life without the organ of a *Watchman*. He succeeds with his murderous scheme, but fails to recognize that the established peace is of artificial nature and not *society-determined*. It is likely to vanish together with his era of *dictatorship*. The genocide of millions New Yorker is ethically not justifiable just as little as his gamble on probabilities about the outcome of his enterprise. Veidt is no hero and in fact, represents the ethically questionable villain who has no respect for life and pursues his egoistic goals of self-realization: the ruler of the world. Nonetheless, "morality begins with the good will" (Loftis 71) – an intention both characters possess; therefore, from an ethical perspective it is hard to denote their actions and conduct as continuously wrong or right. Interestingly enough, an ancient wisdom seems to provide us with a reasonable approach to dismantle the complex issue: "Nobody is perfect".

5. Works Cited

Coogan, Peter. "The Definition of the Superhero". *Superhero: The Secret Origin of a Genre*. Austin: Monkey Brain Books, 2006.

Nuttall, Alex. "When Telling the Truth is Wrong". *Watchmen and Philosophy: A Rorschach Test (The Blackwell Philosophy and Pop Culture Series)*. Ed. **William Irwin** and **Mark D. White**. Indianapolis: Wiley, 2009.

Moore, Alan. *Watchmen*. New York: DC Comics, 2008.

Niebuhr, Reinhold. *Moral Man and Immoral Society: A Study in Ethics and Politics*. Louisville: Westminster John Knox Press, 2002.

Loftis, Robert J. "Means, Ends, and the Critique of Pure Superheroes". *Watchmen and Philosophy: A Rorschach Test (The Blackwell Philosophy and Pop Culture Series)*. Ed.. William Irwin and Mark D. White. Indianapolis: Wiley, 2009.

White, Mark D. "The Virtues of Nite Owl's Potbelly". *Watchmen and Philosophy: A Rorschach Test (The Blackwell Philosophy and Pop Culture Series)*. Ed. William Irwin and Mark D. White. Indianapolis: Wiley, 2009.

Kant, Immanuel. *Groundwork of the Metaphysics of Morals*. Ed. Mary Gregor and Christine M. Korsgaard. Cambridge: Cambridge University Press, 1998 .